C000261882

The Hermetic History Of The Nagas

A. S. Raleigh

Kessinger Publishing's Rare Reprints

Thousands of Scarce and Hard-to-Find Books on These and other Subjects!

- Americana
- Ancient Mysteries
- Animals
- Anthropology
- Architecture
- Arts
- Astrology
- Bibliographies
- Biographies & Memoirs
- Body, Mind & Spirit
- Business & Investing
- Children & Young Adult
- Collectibles
- Comparative Religions
- Crafts & Hobbies
- Earth Sciences
- Education
- Ephemera
- Fiction
- Folklore
- Geography
- Health & Diet
- History
- Hobbies & Leisure
- Humor
- Illustrated Books
- Language & Culture
- Law
- Life Sciences

- Literature
- Medicine & Pharmacy
- Metaphysical
- Music
- Mystery & Crime
- Mythology
- Natural History
- Outdoor & Nature
- Philosophy
- Poetry
- Political Science
- Science
- Psychiatry & Psychology
- Reference
- Religion & Spiritualism
- Rhetoric
- Sacred Books
- Science Fiction
- Science & Technology
- Self-Help
- Social Sciences
- Symbolism
- Theatre & Drama
- Theology
- Travel & Explorations
- War & Military
- Women
- Yoga
- *Plus Much More!*

We kindly invite you to view our catalog list at:
http://www.kessinger.net

THIS ARTICLE WAS EXTRACTED FROM THE BOOK:

Shepherd of Man: An Official Commentary on the
Sermon of Hermes Trismegistos

BY THIS AUTHOR:

A. S. Raleigh

ISBN 1564594939

READ MORE ABOUT THE BOOK AT OUR WEB SITE:

http://www.kessinger.net

OR ORDER THE COMPLETE
BOOK FROM YOUR FAVORITE STORE

ISBN 1564594939

Because this article has been extracted from a parent book, it may have non-pertinent text at the beginning or end of it.

CHAPTER VI.

THE NAGAS.

At the same time that the Mayas settled in Akkad there were other exploring parties that set out for the coasts of Asia. One of these parties, however, sailed westward by way of the Pacific ocean, hence they came from the western portion of Mexico, at a time shortly before the first beginnings of the mighty Toltec race. At this time the Mayas had covered practically all of Mexico and Central America, and as they wished to extend their dominion they sought other countries, and, being the rulers of the sea, they struck right across the Pacific. This was some 13,000 B. C. After a long voyage, lasting for several years, during which they visited several of the islands of the Pacific and established colonies in a great many of them, a portion of the party reached the Dekkan Peninsula, where they established a small settlement. In later times, this settlement became the mighty Naga Empire. They conquered and settled the whole of what in later times was called Hindustan. They gave to themselves the name of Nagas, meaning Snakes, which shows that they were worshippers of the Guchumatz and of Quetzalcoatl. Their king went by the title of Khan. The Nagas extended their conquests westward and northwestward, until the entire territory of southern and western Asia was dominated by them as far as the Akkadian and Chaldean Empire. They settled Burmah and Ceylon, and covered all India and Farther India. We are told in the Ramayana, Hippolite Fauche's Translation, Vol. 1, page 353, that their coming into the country was in times so remote that the Sun had not risen, but we are to bear in mind that the Hindoos had not been in India previous to about 5000 years ago, and hence the Nagas had been there 10,000 years before they came, hence their great antiquity would appeal very strongly to the barbarous Aryans. Their remains are to this day quite visible in Java, where they settled, and left great architectural evidences of their residence. All of those buildings are the exact duplicates in point of style of those in Yucatan, and thus we see the indisputable evidences that the civilization of ancient Java was that of the Nagas.

They extended their sway westward, and settled what is now Afghanistan, Turkestan, Beloochistan, as well as all Persia. The Afghans are their descendants. In 1879 there were Maya tribes speaking the Maya language residing on the banks of the Kabul river, a name which in Mayan means the Miraculous Hand. Throughout all of that section of Asia the major portion of the ancient place names that are still on the map are pure Mayan names, having a distinct meaning in the common language of the Mayas, but being only place names in other languages. For a list of those names and their meaning in Mayan, see the Word, Vol. XVII, No. 1, article, The Origin of the Egyptians, Le Plongeon. All India and Persia and the adjacent countries were dominated by the Nagas, and their great culture spread throughout all southern and western Asia. In the course of time their dominion became so great that it was unwieldy, and in time it was divided into the Southern and Western Empire, though they were the same people. The Southern Empire comprised all India, Burmah, Ceylon, Java Afghanistan and adjacent countries, while the Western Empire comprised Persia and the adjacent territories as far as Akkadia and Chaldea.

Among all the Nagas there was the same form
of government; the king was divine, and ruled
as the Son of the Sun or of the Great Serpent.
He was the visible incarnation on earth of the
Divine Power that was identical with Quetzalcoatl.
Hence his power was absolute and was to be
called in question by no one. Not only was the
king divine, but there was a measure of Divinity
attached to the persons of all in whom flowed the
royal blood. In Persia the doctrine that what-
ever the king willed was right, was the outgrowth
of the ancient belief that he was divine. That the
Serpent or Sun God was manifest in him, and
hence his will was but the individualized form of
the Divine Will. Also, the Mind of the God was
manifest in his mind, and hence all his decisions
were infallible, hence all the decrees that he made
were infallible, and as they in reality emanated
from the Mind of the Serpent God they were as
changeless as He was, therefore the decree of a
king could never be changed, for it had come from
the God, and the God did not change his Mind.
Thus it was that while the king was infallible and
all powerful, yet he could not in the slightest
degree alter any of the decrees of his predeces-
sors. The laws of the country were merely the
body of the decrees of all past kings.

In the course of time human sacrifices became
introduced among the Nagas, both those in India
and also those in Persia. There is a legend of
one of the Persian kings, who had a snake growing
out of each of his shoulders, and that these snakes
had to be fed every day on the hearts of men, and
as they grew there was an ever increasing number
of human hearts that had to be given to them,
so that the country groaned under the scourge.
At last there was an uprising, in which the king
was killed and a new king set up in his place.
The meaning of this story is not hard to dis-

cover. The king was the dynasty at that time. The snakes were the cultus of the Guchumatz and of Quetzalcoatl. Their growing out of the shoulders of the king indicated that the ruling dynasty was devoted to the worship of those deities, and that the royalty was directly connected with the priesthood of the Cultus. The feeding of the hearts of men to the snakes indicates that according to the Cultus at that time these Serpent Gods had to be propitiated with human sacrifice, and that it was only the hearts that were sacrificed to them. Thus it is that we see the necessity for a great number of victims for the altars of those deties. But the question is, Why did they offer the hearts to them in preference to any other portion of the victim? The answer is not difficult to discover. The heart was by many of the Maya nations believed to be the seat of the soul, and the idea was that the Serpent Deities devoured the souls of men. This gruesome Cultus is still surviving in the Shiva Cultus of India, which is the direct survival of the Indian Nagas. Then there was another reason for this practice, the heart is the seat of the emotional nature, and this belongs to the domain of Quetzalcoatl. It is a fundamental Hermetic Doctrine that as one ascends toward his source he must give up the emotions and all the Astral activities, or de-energize those energies, and in this way permit them to return to their source in Quetzalcoatl, and there is no doubt that this sacrifice of the hearts of men was designed to symbolize the interior sacrifice which every man must make of his emotional nature. There grew up in the course of time the idea that inasmuch as the de-energizing of the Astral energies caused them to return into the great supply or Quetzalcoatl, he was nourished thereby, and hence, would suffer if he was not fed regularly in this way. We see identically the same idea current among

the Aztec barbarians in Mexico when they adopted
the Quezalcoatl Cultus. In the course of time
the Nagas reached the conclusion that the sacrifice
of the hearts of men would of itself de-energize
the Astral energies, and we must bear in mind
that this belief is the origin of the practice of
cremation, and that the Hindoos and the Budd-
hists of the Orient believe in it at the present
time. This may be disputed at first, but it can
very easily be proven. They think that so long
as the body continues, the Astral will be bound to
the earth, and that the soul can never reincarnate,
and as reincarnation takes place only upon the
de-energizing of the Astral Shell it follows that
they cremate in order to de-energize the body and
let the Astral go free, and in time it will also
become de-energized. The practise of cremation
was introduced by the Nagas for the purpose of
de-energizing the body, and facilitating the de-
energizing of the Astral, not out of tenderness
for the dead, but in order that Quetzalcoatl might
be nourished upon those energies as they returned
to Him, and the practice of cremation has ever
since been the direct survival of that super-
stition. Now, all this being true, it followed
that if the energies of a dead man were good to
eat, those of a live man were better, and so they
adopted the custom of offering the hearts of men
to the God. Then there grew out of this the idea
that this sacrifice would operate vicariously for
the living, and hence we have the complete Cultus of Human Sacrifice. Of course, the longer
the Cultus stood the more victims were required,
and in the end the toll became unbearable and
there was a revolution in which that dynasty was
overthrown and the Cultus brought to an end.
The practise of human sacrifice was ended and
there was a reformation in the Cultus of Quetzalcoatl and the Guchumatz and they were restored
back to something like their original form.

It was, however, those sanguinary rites and the beliefs associated with them, that formed the sanguinary character of both the Persian and Indian Nagas, and that have survived through their descendants with but few exceptions. Notwithstanding this, however, they were one of the most highly civilized peoples that the world has ever known.